TABLE OF CONTENTS

Sir Walter Raleigh

History Maker Bios

Stephanie Sammartino McPherson

LERNER PUBLICATIONS COMPANY • MINNEAPOLIS

With grateful appreciation, to the librarians of Virginia.

Thanks to my editors Matt Doeden and Megan Moore for help and suggestions and to Richard McPherson and Marion and Angelo Sammartino for reading this manuscript.

There are several different versions of the spelling of Sir Walter Raleigh's last name. Although he generally preferred the spelling "Ralegh," most people are familiar with a different spelling, "Raleigh." That is the form used in this book.

The titles of Raleigh's books appear in modern spelling. We have retained his spelling of "Guiana" to indicate the region he explored.

Illustrations by Tim Parlin

Text copyright © 2005 by Stephanie Sammartino McPherson
Illustrations copyright © 2005 by Lerner Publications Company

Lerner Publications Company
A division of Lerner Publishing Group
241 First Avenue North
Minneapolis, MN 55401   U.S.A.

Website address: www.lernerbooks.com

Library of Congress Cataloging-in-Publication Data

McPherson, Stephanie Sammartino.
    Sir Walter Raleigh / by Stephanie Sammartino McPherson.
        p.   cm. — (History maker bios)
    Includes bibliographical references (p.) and index.
    ISBN-13: 978-0-8225-2945-3 (lib. bdg. : alk. paper)
    ISBN-10: 0-8225-2945-9 (lib. bdg. : alk. paper)
    1. Raleigh, Walter, Sir, 1552?–1618—Juvenile literature. 2. Great Britain—
Court and courtiers—Biography—Juvenile literature. 3. Explorers—Great
Britain—Biography—Juvenile literature. I. Title. II. Series.
DA86.22.R2M385 2005
942.05'5'092—dc22   2004028894

Manufactured in the United States of America
1 2 3 4 5 6 – JR – 10 09 08 07 06 05

INTRODUCTION

Sir Walter Raleigh had more adventures in his lifetime than most people even imagine. He was a soldier, poet, and protector of Queen Elizabeth I of England. He was also a scientist, an explorer, and even a pirate.

The newly discovered lands of the Americas, with their promise of riches and opportunities, fascinated Walter. He started the first English settlement in the New World and helped lead the way to starting the colonies that later became part of the United States of America.

This is his story.

1 LONGING FOR ADVENTURE

Walter Raleigh was a farmer's son. He grew up in a thatched-roof cottage in the southeast part of England. The ocean was not far away. It called to an adventure-loving boy like Walter.

Young Walter had two half brothers from his father's family and three more from his mother's. He also had an older brother named Carew and a sister named Margery.

Little is known about Walter's early days—not even the year of his birth. Some historians think he was born in 1552. Others guess as late as 1554. Walter probably spent time hunting, fishing, and helping on the farm. He loved the land that his parents rented in the county of Devon.

Walter had a restless side too. Humphrey Gilbert, Walter's half brother, encouraged Walter's sense of adventure. Passing sailors also enchanted Walter with tales of distant lands.

Walter's half brother, Humphrey Gilbert, (RIGHT) was an adventurer and explorer.

By 1572, Walter was attending college at Oxford. He liked books and science, but he didn't stay to finish school. Instead, he went to London. He hoped to meet powerful people and become important himself.

Humphrey also lived in London. In June 1578, Queen Elizabeth gave Humphrey the right to explore new lands and claim them for England. Spain had already claimed land in the Americas, which Europeans called the New World. Humphrey hoped that finding new lands would make him rich and make England stronger.

A VERY YOUNG SOLDIER

When Walter was fourteen, one of his cousins called for volunteers to help fight a religious war in France. Walter went with his cousin to defend his faith. But Walter was shocked by the cruelty of both sides of the war. He decided that the battles were really about power, not religion.

Battles between English and Spanish ships were common in the late 1500s.

Walter was only twenty-four years old when he set sail as a commander in his brother's fleet of ships. Strong winds forced most of the ships home. But Walter kept going until he came across several Spanish ships. England and Spain were enemies, and a battle started. Walter's ship was badly damaged. Many of his men died. He was lucky to return home alive.

Walter had to find another way to prove his value to his country. England had some colonies in nearby Ireland. To start the colonies, the English had taken land from people who had lived there for centuries. The Irish were determined to drive the English off their lands. In 1580, Walter sailed to Ireland to fight for England.

Once Walter's group of soldiers was attacked near a river. Walter escaped by crossing the river, but his friend Henry Moyle was captured. Walter quickly jumped back into the river. He fought off Henry's captors with a pistol and stick. Finally, more English soldiers arrived to rescue them. Walter was a hero.

2 CLIMBING HIGH

When Walter returned to London in 1581, he was eager to make his mark in the royal court. He was handsome, charming, and clever—exactly the kind of man to capture the attention of Queen Elizabeth.

This portrait of Queen Elizabeth was painted in the 1580s.

According to one famous story, Walter met the queen as she walked across some wet ground. He threw his cloak onto the ground for her to walk on so she wouldn't get her feet muddy. Another story describes how Walter wanted to catch Elizabeth's attention. Walter used a diamond to scratch a message to her onto a window. He said he wanted to climb hish in her service. The queen did remember Walter. She gave him gifts and special rights.

Walter could tax winemakers and wool merchants and keep some of the money he collected. The queen even let him live in a mansion called Durham House. In return, Walter wrote poems to honor her.

Walter led a good life. He had many friends. He had enough money to pay for the fine clothes he loved. He was even able to help pay for Humphrey's next voyage.

Sadly, Humphrey was lost at sea and never returned. But Walter wasn't ready to give up. He asked the queen for the same honor she had given Humphrey—the right to search for and claim new lands.

Walter enjoyed life in the royal court.

Even before she agreed, Walter was getting his ships ready. He studied maps and learned about sailing routes. He prepared himself for the journey. But later, the queen decided that she couldn't spare Walter for the trip. On April 27, 1584, the ships left without him. The crew would explore new lands and report on the best spot for a colony.

Two Native Americans from the New World sailed back with Walter's fleet to England. Walter welcomed them and the ship's captain to Durham House. He listened as Captain Arthur Barlowe talked about the New World and the land called Virginia.

This map of Virginia was made in 1588.

Walter's importance grew. He became a member of Parliament, the group that made England's laws. On January 6, 1585, the queen made him a knight. His new title was Sir Walter Raleigh, Knight Lord and Governor of Virginia.

As he planned his next voyage, Walter was determined to see Virginia for himself. He was eager to start the first English settlement in the New World.

WHAT'S IN A NAME?

The first Europeans to sail to the New World thought they had reached the Indies. That was why they called the people there "Indians." Walter's first explorers thought that the Indians called their land Wingandacoa. Later, Walter's friend Thomas Harriot learned that the word really meant, "You have fine clothes." Walter and the queen agreed to name the land Virginia after Elizabeth, who was called "the Virgin Queen."

3 AN APPETITE FOR POWER

Again, Queen Elizabeth spoiled Walter's big plans to sail to Virginia. She refused to let him leave her side. Walter's cousin, Sir Richard Grenville, took his place on the voyage.

Six ships set sail on April 9, 1585. About one hundred men had promised to stay in the New World when the ships returned home. Under the leadership of Ralph Lane, the men would start a colony on Roanoke Island.

Despite the settlers' efforts, the colony didn't do well. The colonists depended on Indians for most of their food. But during the winter, the Indians didn't have enough food for everyone. When the famous explorer Sir Francis Drake visited the settlement, most of the men returned with him to England.

Sir Francis Drake led the second voyage around the world from 1577 to 1580.

Walter's colony had barely lasted a year. The settlers hadn't found gold or jewels, as they'd hoped. But Virginia had valuable cedar trees and sassafras. This plant was thought to cure some diseases. Virginia was also rich in tobacco, a plant that the Indians smoked in long pipes.

Walter thought that he could convince people to try smoking. He hoped that he would be able to sell them tobacco. One story tells that when Walter tried a pipe, a servant saw him blow smoke from his mouth. The servant thought Walter was on fire, so he threw a bucket of water in his face!

Walter brought back tobacco from Virginia and introduced Europeans to the idea of smoking.

Walter had many things to think about besides the New World. The queen had put him in charge of several tin mines. She had also appointed him admiral of the West. His job was to keep all the ships under his control in fighting condition. This was important because relations between England and Spain were getting worse. Many people expected a war to start soon.

PIRATES ON THE HIGH SEAS

In the years leading up to war with Spain, many English ship captains seized ships from Spain and other countries. Walter owned several of these English ships. His sailors stole jewels, spices, fish, salt, and grain. They then brought the loot back to England. Queen Elizabeth herself approved. She began giving these pirate sailors permission to raid ships. She called them "voluntaries."

Meanwhile, Walter received his greatest honor. In 1586, Elizabeth named him captain of the guard. At the age of thirty-three, Walter was responsible for the queen's safety at all times. He rarely left her side.

Despite his duties, Walter found time to plan another trip to Virginia. For a year, he'd thought about what had happened in Roanoke. Walter wanted his new settlers to consider the colony their home. That didn't seem likely in a group made up of just men. This time, he would send colonists with wives and children.

On July 22, 1587, Walter's colonists arrived in Roanoke. Soon a baby was born. Her parents named her Virginia. Walter's plan had worked. The settlers considered the colony their home.

Although the settlers were busy and happy, they needed more supplies, especially salt and cattle. Someone had to sail to England with the colony's requests, but no one wanted to leave. Finally, the head of the colony, an artist named John White, said he would make the trip.

Virginia Dare, the first English child born in the New World, was baptized at Roanoke in 1587.

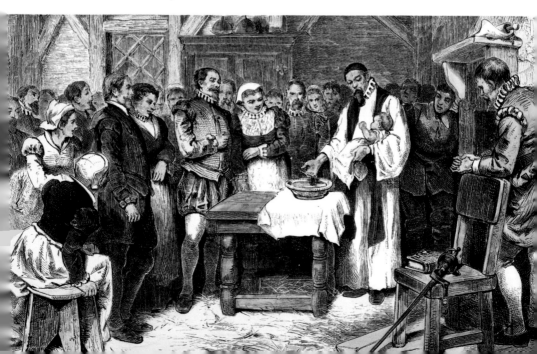

In England, Walter had other problems. The queen had placed him on the Council of War. This council helped prepare for a possible war with Spain. Walter's job was to raise troops and defend coastlines. It was a huge responsibility. Luckily, Walter had an appetite for power. He thrived on all he had to do.

With the war likely to start at any time, Walter couldn't help the Virginia settlement. He listened to John White's requests. Then he tried to send supplies, but his small ships were forced to return. The colonists would have to wait.

4 IN AND OUT OF FAVOR

In July 1588, Spain sent a fleet of warships toward England. The Spanish Armada included more than 130 ships and 2,500 guns. Walter was ready. Under his direction, lanterns flashed along the coast to warn of the enemy's arrival.

English sailors weren't willing to just wait for the Armada to attack. They had a plan. Sailors set fire to some of their own ships. They sent them floating out toward the enemy ships.

The Spanish captains panicked. They turned their ships away from the fires and toward the North Sea. They never even attacked. Storms and high winds in the North Sea sank many of the Spanish ships. The Spanish Armada did not return to England.

The defeat of the Spanish Armada was a great victory for England.

When John White returned to Virginia, he found the colony deserted.

After the battle, Walter sent John White with three supply ships back to Virginia. But by the time they arrived in August of 1590, the colonists had vanished. The colony was overgrown with weeds. The mystery of the lost colony has never been completely solved.

The queen was getting tired of the failed attempts to start colonies in the New World. She thought it made more sense to start colonies closer to home. She gave Walter large pieces of land in Ireland. There, he started the English community of Munster.

When Elizabeth Throckmorton married Walter, she became Lady Raleigh.

In late 1591, Walter secretly married a young woman named Elizabeth (Bess) Throckmorton. Bess was one of Queen Elizabeth's ladies-in-waiting. These servants lived with the queen at court and took care of her needs.

Bess told no one of her marriage. Later, she gave birth to a son, Damerei. Soon, she returned to court as if nothing had happened.

Queen Elizabeth wasn't fooled. The queen wanted everyone's complete devotion. As far as she was concerned, that ruled out romance. Furious, she placed Walter and his bride under house arrest.

Although the queen was angry, she still cared about Walter. She didn't know what to do next. To reward Walter for his past service, she gave him a country home called Sherborne. But she could not forgive him for his marriage. Instead of letting the young couple enjoy Sherborne, she moved them to the famous prison known as the Tower of London.

These are ruins of the castle that the queen gave Walter. He lived here for a few years before building a new home on the estate. He called it Sherborne Lodge.

Walter would do anything to regain the queen's favor. Soon one of his ships gave him a chance. Walter's ship captured a Portuguese vessel that carried great treasure. When the Portuguese ship was brought into port, villagers swarmed aboard. They took pearls, precious metals, and spices. The sailors couldn't stop them. The queen was in danger of losing her share of the riches.

Walter owned several ships. One of the most famous was the ARK ROYAL. Queen Elizabeth later bought it from him.

Winning back Queen Elizabeth's favor was hard for Walter.

Finally, the queen asked Walter to save the treasure. Under his command, the sailors stopped the looting and took back some of the stolen goods.

The queen was grateful. She freed Walter and his wife in time for Christmas. But she was still angry and did not allow them back into her court. She took away Walter's right to gather tax money from the wine and wool industries. For Walter to regain the queen's favor, he had to do more than rescue some treasure.

Walter wanted to explore the lush green lands of South America.

For years, Walter had been fascinated by tales of El Dorado. This legendary city of gold was said to be in the South American kingdom of Guiana. People said that the city was so rich that the king and his servants covered their bodies with gold dust. Walter wanted to find the city and claim it for England. If he did, the queen would have to forgive him and take him back into her court.

On February 6, 1595, Walter set sail with a fleet of six ships. On the Caribbean island of Trinidad, he captured a Spanish explorer who was also looking for El Dorado. Walter learned what he could from the man. Then Walter and his crew explored the mainland of South America.

The group's supplies quickly ran low. But a local leader, or cacique, gave Walter enough food and drink for everyone. Walter tried to meet as many caciques as he could. He made sure his men behaved fairly and respectfully toward the people they met.

Many sailors feared they would run into sea serpents in their journeys to the strange lands across the Atlantic Ocean.

Walter didn't find El Dorado. But he passed through beautiful countryside on his way up the Orinoco River. He gathered stories about strange people. He learned of a huge silver mine and collected stones that he thought contained gold. Most of all, he experienced the sights and sounds of the New World.

WALTER, THE TRAVEL WRITER

Some people doubted Walter's amazing tales of South America. They accused him of hiding in England while pretending to cross the ocean. In response, Walter wrote about Guiana, the place we know as the countries of Venezuela and Guyana. He described the land and the natives, his hardships, and his hopes of future riches. *The Discovery of the Large, Rich, and Beautiful Empire of Guiana* was immediately popular. Even playwright William Shakespeare took note of Walter's book.

The queen wanted riches—not stories—from these journeys. She wasn't ready to forgive Walter yet. Still, Walter remained loyal. He fought bravely in England's attack on the Spanish port of Cádiz. He even helped make the battle plan that led to an English victory.

Many of Walter's powerful friends asked the queen to forgive him. Finally, she gave up her grudge. On July 1, 1597, six years after his marriage, Walter was welcomed back to the royal court.

5 BRAVE TO THE END

Walter served the queen for more than five years. Her death on March 24, 1603, was a terrible blow. The new king, James I, didn't trust Walter. A member of Queen Elizabeth's court had already spoken against Walter. The new king didn't want anyone else around who could challenge his power.

Walter lost his position as captain of the guard. His home at Durham House was taken away. But none of this prepared him for what happened next. He was arrested and locked in the Tower of London.

Several months later, Walter was put on trial for trying to overthrow the king. Prisoners had few rights in the early 1600s. In modern times, someone accused of a crime is innocent until proven guilty. Walter faced the opposite situation. He was considered guilty until he proved his innocence.

James I of England

Walter believed a man should have the right to face his accuser. He said that a person should only be found guilty if two witnesses spoke against that person. People who watched the trial thought about these new ideas. As the trial went on, many people began to agree with Walter.

The judges, however, didn't agree. Walter was found guilty and sentenced to death. He hoped that the king would change his sentence. But Walter prepared to die.

Walter was held prisoner in the Tower of London during and after his trial.

Walter's young son often visited him in the Tower of London. Wat later joined Walter on his voyages.

King James kept Walter in doubt until the last moment. Finally, on the day that he was to be executed, the news came. Walter's life was spared.

Fifty-year-old Walter was treated well in prison. He had two comfortable rooms and three servants. Bess and their ten-year-old son, Wat, often stayed with him. Another son, Carew, was born in 1605.

Queen Anne personally thanked Walter for helping her recover from an illness.

Walter grew herbs and tobacco in his own garden plot and did scientific experiments in a shed. He made a famous medicine he called his cordial. The king's wife, Queen Anne, was ill and tried his medicine. After recovering, she went to the prison to thank Walter.

The queen enjoyed Walter's company. She later brought her son, Prince Henry, to meet him. Henry was nothing like his father. He knew that Walter could teach him about science, history, and politics. Soon Walter became the prince's tutor.

For many years, Walter had thought about writing a book on the history of the world. He began the great book for Henry. It would be made up of several separate books, or volumes. As he wrote, he shared ideas and read passages to the prince.

Many people consider the first volume of *History of the World* to be a masterpiece. But before Walter could begin the next two books, Prince Henry died—probably of a disease called typhoid. Walter was heartbroken. He lost all interest in his history.

While in prison, Walter did his writing at this desk.

If Henry had lived, the young prince might have helped Walter gain his freedom. Now Walter had to rely on himself. After thirteen years in prison, Walter convinced James I to let him make another trip to South America. He promised to find a gold mine for the king.

During the long voyage, Walter became ill. By the time he reached South America, he was too weak to seek a gold mine. Instead of leaving the ship himself, he sent out exploring parties in small boats.

Walter was too sick to join his crew in the exploration of the South American jungle.

Walter could hardly wait for word of their discoveries. But instead, Walter got terrible news. The men had not found a mine. Much worse, they had disobeyed the king's orders. They had fought the Spanish, who were also exploring the area. During the fight, Wat had been killed. So had some Spanish soldiers.

Walter was sick with grief. He had lost everything—his son, his fortune, and his future. He knew that he faced death for disobeying the king. But instead of escaping, Walter returned to England.

AN UNJUST KING

King James wanted Walter to fail. As Walter prepared for his final voyage, the king ordered him not to fight with any Spaniards. Walter didn't know that the king had told the Spanish government exactly what Walter's plans were. When Walter set out for Guiana, the Spanish settlers in South America were already expecting him. Walter wouldn't be able to avoid a fight. Then the king would have a reason to order his death.

On the day of his death, Walter gave his hat to an old man. "You need more of it now than I," he joked. As Walter stood outside the Tower of London before his death, he gave a long speech. He wanted to be sure that everyone knew that he was innocent.

The people who heard Walter were deeply moved. Even the man who was to kill him hesitated to act. "Strike, man, strike," Walter said. The axe came down on his neck. He died on October 29, 1618.

Walter was beheaded on October 29, 1618.

Walter's life was an amazing series of ups and downs. His American settlements failed. But he sparked the interest that led to a permanent colony. He did not discover El Dorado. But he wrote a brilliant book about his travels that became a best seller. He lost his trial, but he raised important points about justice and English law. Whatever his disappointments, Walter always sprang back with new plans. His courage and determination helped shape history.

TIMELINE

WALTER WAS PROBABLY
BORN BETWEEN 1552
AND 1554.

In the year . . .

1568 Walter fought alongside the Protestants in France. *Age 14*

1578 he set sail as a commander in his half brother Humphrey's fleet.

1580 Walter fought in Ireland.

1584 he sent a fleet to explore the coast of North America.

1585 he was knighted by Queen Elizabeth I. *Age 31*
he sent out a fleet to establish a colony in Virginia.

1586 he was made captain of the guard.

1587 he sent ships to start another colony in Virginia.

1591 he secretly married Elizabeth (Bess) Throckmorton.

1592 his son Damerei was born.
Walter was banished from court.

1593 his son Wat was born.

1595 Walter set out to find El Dorado. *Age 41*

1597 he was received back into the royal court.

1603 Elizabeth I died.
he was tried and convicted of treason against *Age 49*
King James I.

1605 Walter's son Carew was born.

1614 the first volume of Walter's *History of the World* was published.

1617 he led another expedition to Guiana. *Age 63*
Wat was killed in a battle in Guiana.

1618 Walter was put to death in London.

What Happened
to the Lost Colonists?

Did the lost colonists leave clues for Governor John White? On arriving in Roanoke from England, White discovered the letters CRO on a tree. He also found the word CROATOAN written on a post. White believed these letters were messages from the colonists saying that they had sailed to the island of Croatoan.

Historians have several ideas about what happened to the lost colonists. Disease might have killed them. They might have tried to sail back to England and been lost at sea.

One idea is especially interesting. The colonists in Jamestown, England's first permanent colony in the New World, heard stories about white settlers who had married Native Americans. Almost four hundred years later, some members of the Croatoan tribe have blue eyes and light hair. They could be descendants of the lost colonists.

FURTHER READING

NONFICTION

Fisher, Leonard Everett. *The Tower of London*. New York: Macmillan Publishing Company, 1987. Illustrated in black and white, this book presents the history of London's famous prison.

Yolen, Jane, and Heidi Elisabet Yolen Stemple. *Roanoke, The Lost Colony: An Unsolved Mystery from History*. New York: Simon and Schuster, 2003. Eye-catching illustrations and historical clues invite the reader to solve the mystery of the lost colony.

FICTION

Lasky, Kathryn. *Elizabeth I: Red Rose of the House of Tudor, 1544*. New York: Scholastic, 2002. This is a fictional diary of the young woman who became England's beloved queen.

Sewall, Marcia. *James Towne: Struggle for Survival*. New York: Atheneum Books for Young Readers, 2001. This picture book tells the story of England's first permanent colony in the New World through the fictionalized journal of one of its settlers.

WEBSITES

Elizabeth's Pirates
http://www.channel4.com/history/microsites/H/history /pirates/index.html This website provides interesting information about sixteenth-century piracy and about the invasion of the Spanish Armada.

Fort Raleigh National Historic Site
http://www.nps.gov/fora/children.htm This is the website
for the national park that is on the site of Walter's lost
colony near what is now Manteo, North Carolina. The
website includes a children's page.

Sir Walter Raleigh, of Hayes Barton, Woodbury Common
http://www.btinternet.com/~richard.towers/jim/raleigh.html
Hayes Barton, the farmhouse where Walter was born, still
stands in Devon, England. This website includes
information on Raleigh's early life, his poetry, the Spanish
Armada, and the Tower of London.

SELECT BIBLIOGRAPHY

Aronson, Marc. *Sir Walter Ralegh and the Quest for El
Dorado.* New York: Clarion Books, 2000.

Beer, Anna. *My Just Desire: The Life of Bess Ralegh, Wife
to Sir Walter.* New York: Ballantine Books, 2003.

Lacey, Robert. *Sir Walter Ralegh.* London: Phoenix Press,
2000. First published 1973 by Weidenfelt and Nicolson.

Shirley, John W. *Sir Walter Ralegh and the New World.*
Raleigh, NC: North Carolina Division of Archives and
History, 1985.

Stick, David. *Roanoke Island: The Beginnings of English
America.* Chapel Hill: University of North Carolina Press,
1983.

Trevelyan, Raleigh. *Sir Walter Raleigh.* New York: Henry
Holt and Company, 2002.

INDEX

Acknowledgments

For photographs and artwork: Dictionary of American Portraits, p. 4; © Getty Images, pp. 7; © North Wind Picture Archives, pp. 9, 14, 21, 24, 25, 40, 45; © SuperStock, Inc./ SuperStock, pp. 12, 31; © Culver Pictures, Inc./SuperStock, p. 13; Library of Congress, pp. 17 (LC-USZ62-38479), 35 (LC-USZ67-62341), 36 (LC-USZ61-942); © Charles Marden Fitch/SuperStock, p. 18; © Brown Brothers, p. 20; © The Granger Collection, New York, pp. 26, 37; © Rosemary Calvert/ SuperStock, p. 27; Mary Evans Picture Library, p. 28, 42; © Francis G. Mayer/CORBIS, p. 29; © Charles & Josette Lenars/CORBIS, p. 30; © Historical Picture Archive/CORBIS, p. 38; © Nancy Carter/North Wind Picture Archives, p. 39. **Front cover:** Courtesy of The North Carolina State Archive. **Back cover:** © North Wind Picture Archives.

For quoted material: p. 42, Raleigh Trevelyan, *Sir Walter Raleigh* (New York: Henry Holt and Company, 2002); p. 42, Robert Lacey, *Sir Walter Ralegh* (London: Phoenix Press, 2000).